ACKNOWLEDGEMENT

I want to acknowledge my dear friend Mark Snowden for his contribution as editor on this project. Over the years Mark and I have worked on several projects and my respect and admiration for him grows with every year of our association. Thank you Mark.

My respect and love for my wife Gailia and our daughter Amber has grown during our time in Iraq. These two special ladies have freed me to fulfill my role and service to our Great God and King. They are *troopers*—enduring hardship and personal sacrifice. Both Gailia and Amber have helped make me the man I am. Thank you my dear girls. I love you.

Also, I want to thank my brother Greg Smith for his work on the cover design. His patience and willingness to demonstrate creativity and make necessary changes when I asked for them has increased my love and appreciation for him exponentially. He is a true servant. Thank you brother!

Between Two Rivers

C. Brandt Smith, Jr.

For information:

Brandt Smith Publishing
3501 Ridgeway Circle
Jonesboro, Arkansas 72404
Email: info@bsp.com

Printed in the United States of America
Between Two Rivers / C. Brandt Smith, Jr.

ISBN 0-9768020-1-5
Printed in U.S. by
www.brandtsmithpublishing.com

Contents

—Prologue—

My heart has never been as grieved as it has been over the people who live in the city of Baghdad. Over the past 15 years, our family has lived in several cities around the world. There have been cities with populations of greater than 12 million and cities with populations as few as in the thousands. We have invested our lives learning culture, language, and the local customs. We have always been challenged beyond what most people are willing to endure.

Living in Baghdad, Iraq's largest city and the nation's

capitol, has been very challenging and even more difficult than anything we've ever experienced. During our first 15 months, I lost dozens of friends due to the violence and chaos that has become commonplace in this dangerous city. When my list reached 76 names, I could no longer bring myself to record the names of Iraqis I personally knew who had been killed by assassination, random shootings, and car bombs. It just hurt too deeply to keep recording those names.

The following stories are of people I know, or knew. Their faces are etched forever in my heart and their memories will remain with me long after I leave Iraq. Some of these stories are of God's miraculous protection while other stories are of senseless acts that resulted in death.

My purpose in writing this book is to give you, my readers, a chance to see the plight of the Iraqi people. They are just like you and me—loving parents, students full of potential, and businesspeople interested in making a living. Some of my stories are of Christians, while other stories are of Muslims who never came to a saving knowledge of Jesus Christ.

Chapter One
Terrorist Threat in Sadr City

The cell phone in my pocket surprised me when it began to ring. I noticed the name on the screen as that of one of my project leaders. I never know what the news may be when I receive a call on a Friday. Fridays are considered holidays. In Iraq, even Christians don't work on Fridays.

I answered the call in Arabic, "Hello, hello. *Habibi. Ashlosnik*?" ("Hello, hello. Brother, how are you?")

My project leader sounded disturbed and asked if he could meet with me to talk about a problem.

"Where are you?" I asked. "Are you nearby?"

"Yes," he replied. "Can I come now to talk with you?"

"Sure," I said. "I'll be waiting for you at the checkpoint."

When I saw him, he was walking—almost running—toward my vehicle and quickly jumped into the car.

We were quickly off to the *mahad* (office).

"What is wrong?" I asked. "Are you okay?"

He said he had been out in Sadr City. He was conducting a site survey for a relief and development project—routine stuff. At least until he was informed of several terrorists associated with the Al Sadr

Mahdi Army who had been going into the homes of the people he was trying to care for. They were infiltrating his friends by providing food and medicine.

As he began to tell me of his concerns, it became clear to me that the very people we were trying to help were now being targeted by these men. And the Al Sadr Mahdi Army had a vicious reputation. They would enter the homes of the poorest and most helpless. They demanded to know who was providing them with assistance. And they always wanted to know the location of the office of aid organizations.

My project leader--we'll call him Hussein to protect his identity--said, "If we don't stop these terrorists, they will slaughter many of the people now looking to us for their daily physical needs."

Thoughts raced through my mind as I asked Hussein what he wanted me to do.

"Quickly," he said, "We must contact the coalition forces and let them know where these terrorists are hiding so they can capture them and prevent the deaths of all my people."

After arriving at the *mahad,* we sat down together and we prayed.

Hussein is a new Christian and believes he is called to become a pastor. His religious background is Islam. But now he is gladly serving Jesus.

His compassion for people is amazing. He really loves them and is such a peacemaker. Now he was pleading with me to help him capture terrorists!

As we prayed together the only thing that came to my mind

was the name of a man I had met in Baghdad who said he was connected to the coalition forces. This contact had been in my home many times, eaten meals with our family, and had become a close, personal friend. Maybe he would know what course of action two civilians could take to prevent the murder of many innocent Iraqis.

After our time of prayer, with Hussein looking over my shoulder, I emailed my friend asking him for advice. The answer I received was dreadful to even consider. He wanted me to provide location coordinates by pinpointing these terrorist cells using the Google Earth software that came with my laptop.

So, Hussein began to show me on the computer map where the hideouts were located. One was in a vacant school building; the others in abandoned houses that dotted around a section of Sadr City.

The area where the vacant school was located had become dangerous. The children were unable to attend classes. The parents of these children were told not to send their children to school anymore or they would be killed in their classrooms.

This is a favorite strategy of Al Qaeda terrorists. One of their tactics is to "dumb down" the society by threatening to kill school teachers, principals, and children who desire to gain an education.

The longitude and latitude coordinates were plotted and placed in my next email to my military friend.

The next series of longitude and latitude coordinates showed the actual sites where these Al Qaeda-Mahdi Army terrorists would hide in between their raiding and killing sprees.

There were five locations identified and sent to my military friend for his follow-up. What happened over the next few days was incredible.

Coalition forces had been in the area many times only to come up short capturing these men. Every time coalition forces got close, the terrorists were tipped off and escaped capture.

Gun battle, a repeated scene in Iraq

Hussein let me know some time later that terrorists would actually be hiding in the houses as coalition forces searched for them. I asked Hussein how they could evade capture when the military was so close—even in the same building or house. He let me know that the terrorists would threaten to kill the occupants the very moment the soldiers left if they turned them in. Some hid in the oversized Iraqi ovens right under the top cooking surfaces to evade capture.

And Hussein added with an ominous tone, "Even if some of them were captured, other terrorists would come back to the house after coalition forces left and kill the occupants."

Fear causes people to react in different ways.

Within the next few days, reports of several raids by

coalition forces netted numerous captures and several local residents were saved from being threatened and killed. Others were not so fortunate.

These were the kind of incidents that happened in the neighborhood that caused great pain and suffering. But afterward, Hussein reported to me that stability in the neighborhood greatly improved as dozens of terrorists were captured and other terrorists were no longer able to stay in the area. They simply moved on to other neighborhoods to carry out their activities.

Pray*—Dear Heavenly Father, only You can provide the care and safety the Iraqi people need. Only You can truly save them from the enemy. Only You can meet the deepest needs of their hearts.*

Read—*Psalm 20:7, "Some boast in chariots, and some in horses; But we will boast in the name of the Lord our God."*

Your Thoughts—

____

____

____

____

____

____

____

____

____

____

Chapter Two
Kidnapped and Released

August 1, 2007, my wife, Gailia, my daughter, Amber, and I were on our way out of Iraq traveling to Amman, Jordan, for a few days before traveling onward to Oman. The drive from our home and office should be an easy drive of about twenty minutes. Traffic usually moves well.

However, the road to the Baghdad airport is littered with debris from dozens of cars that have been abandoned after being caught in ambushes. They are pushed to the side and traffic flows around them at a snail's pace. There are also several checkpoints between the office and the Baghdad airport. This also slows down the traffic.

Traveling to the Baghdad airport often takes up to two hours on a good day and is still very dangerous. The route has been called the Shooting Gallery by locals, which only makes a very stressful drive that much worse.

Once inside the airport one begins to feel the heat from lack of air conditioning and hundreds of Iraqis trying to get out of the city. It is a sight we will never forget. Their desperation remains etched upon our memories.

Families huddled together are strongest image. Mothers and fathers struggle to carry all they can have with them. Children in tow can sense the urgency to keep moving. Each step forward helps them make their way to any country who will receive them.

On this particular day, I was standing in line to get our boarding passes and check our luggage only to be told the ticket counter was now closed. I told the counter personnel we had three tickets purchased for the 12:30 flight to Amman and needed to get on that flight.

I was told the jet only had two seats left and I was late to check in. I asked how this could be since I was still an hour and a half early. It didn't matter—the ticket counter was closed. Our seats had been given to others trying to get out of Baghdad.

When I turned around to let Gailia and Amber know our situation, I saw the dismay on their faces. They knew we were not getting on that flight.

There is something emotional that happens to a person when they think they are getting out of Baghdad, even if just for a brief time. The feelings of fear, joy, sadness, and despair are common. The look on Gailia and Amber's faces just killed me. It did not matter that this happens almost every time we try to leave.

But this time it turned out to be a blessing. As I was watching their faces, a man walked up to me and greeted me with three kisses on my cheeks. He asked if I remembered him. I looked into his eyes and instantly knew who he was even though I hadn't seen him in months.

His name was Ali. He had been a prominent lawyer in Baghdad and had been a guest in my home. We were introduced by a Muslim background believer over a meal at my table. I remembered him being jovial and full of energy. Now, in front of me was a man whose eyes were filled with fear and sadness.

I noticed his bandaged arm and the trembling words falling from his lips. I asked Ali what had happened and why he looked so nervous. I was shocked, but not surprised by his answer.

He began to tell me of attempts on his life by the terrorists in Baghdad. He had narrowly escaped several attempts to assassinate him. He explained how these attempts had failed. But now, standing in front of me, he began to relate how he had been taken hostage by some very cruel men and almost lost his life.

As a lawyer, he had taken part in several high profile cases involving the old Sadaam

Hussein regime that used to rule Iraq. His job was to bring to justice the tyrants who had caused so much pain during the years of Sadaam's dictatorship.

However, living in a society that carries grudges from one generation to the next, he was in trouble—big trouble. His home was watched night and day by these terrorists who were willing to wait for an opportune moment to kill him or kidnap him.

Ali told me he had not gone out of his home for weeks and his visit to my home had been a rare event. One of Gailia's great meals, for which she has become famous in our neighborhood, had given him great satisfaction.

Then came the day he needed to leave his home and travel out to renew his license to practice law. The trip to the government office was uneventful. He renewed his credentials and was on his way home when a car pulled alongside his vehicle. He was forced to stop against the curbing.

Several men with weapons pulled him from his car, pushed him into the trunk of their vehicle, and drove away. He said the fear was intense. He knew he would not be allowed to live after reaching their hiding place.

He had been shot through his left arm at close range, shattering the bones. He was so tightly bound by the wires used to incarcerate him that his wrists were scarred and nerves were damaged. He showed me the back of his neck where he had been hung for hours, barely able to stand on his toes, leaving a large swipe of a scar around his neck.

I asked him if he had escaped or how he came to be free.

Ali told me after weeks of negotiation, his family was able to come up with a ransom for his release that totaled $100,000.

Unfortunately, this huge ransom was just the beginning. Next, the terrorists had demanded that regular payments of several thousand dollars be paid to them every month for an unspecified time.

"We are ruined," Ali said. "My mother and father, brothers and sisters are all living in more fear."

Ali was at the airport trying to get out of Baghdad where he thought he could recover from his ordeal. He would live with a family member up north as long as he felt he was safe from his captors. However, his family still living in Baghdad was not safe.

I placed my two hands on this Muslim man's shoulders and shared with him that knowing Jesus was truly his only hope. He could know for sure that when death came to him, he would be eternally free from fear and alive spiritually for all eternity.

We had prayer together that day at the airport and I saw a glimmer of hope return to the eyes of Ali. Coming from a Muslim background and being presented with the claims of Christ were difficult for him to grasp.

He didn't pray to receive Christ that day, but he heard a clear presentation of the gospel. Ali told me I had given him a lot to consider and he was open to what he had heard. He just needed to get out of Baghdad in order to think clearly.

I let Ali know that I was

available to talk further with him. I promised to come up north to spend time with him if he wanted me to drop by. He hugged me and whispered in my ear, "Be careful my American friend. You can't trust anyone."

As I have thought about that meeting with Ali, I wondered, how can someone come so close to death, live through it, and still reject the claims of Jesus Christ? I have no answer for this question. It is a mystery to me.

Pray*—Dear Heavenly Father, please lift the veil of darkness from the eyes of the Iraqis who are trapped in Islam. Allow them to hear with understanding ears Your message of redemption, grace, and mercy. They are lost and don't even know their spiritual condition.*

Read—*Psalm 56:3-4, "When I am afraid, I will put my trust in Thee. In God, whose word I praise, in God I have put my trust; I shall not be afraid. What can mere man do to me?"*

Your Thoughts—

____

____

____

____

____

____

____

____

Chapter Three
Protected by Almighty God

Travel in Baghdad is difficult and at best a risk. However, being called by God to work in this environment has increased the fervor of my prayer life. It has galvanized within me a desire to live every day to the fullest.

One of the tasks I often am called upon to perform is leading workshops and training events around the city. Getting to the site where these workshops are held presents special problems. It takes driving strategies to minimize the danger of being out there "in population."

Most of the time things go well and with the exception of slow traffic and multiple checkpoints, we come and go with what we jokingly call, "Baghdad Normal."

Several months ago, I had been asked to provide some leadership training in an area near our office. The drive would take about 15 minutes if traffic moved and I'd be in and out quickly—safe and sound—at least that was the plan.

On that particular morning, I dressed in my sports jacket and was wearing a necktie. I wanted to look the part of being professional and wanted to make a good impression on my audience.

As a rule, I don't drive in

Baghdad, except on rare occasions. I love to drive, but my company provides a driver for security reasons, who navigates through the barricades, potholes, and checkpoints. All I have to do is sit in the front passenger's seat, hang on, and pray.

Something was different this morning and traffic was, well, let's call it weird. As my driver drove down the main street to our destination, he began to speak in Arabic to my personal assistant who was seated in the back seat of the car.

There was a noticeable, but slight irritation in their voices, but I continued to sit quietly, still praying. As our car approached a "new" checkpoint, a man in uniform stuck his head inside the driver's window and asked a question. My driver said nothing, but handed the soldier his identification card. We were allowed to proceed, but the mood had changed in the car as my driver and personal assistant chattered back and forth.

Curiosity got the best of me and I asked what had just happened. My driver said, “Well, the militia member was searching for members of the Iraqi Ministry of Planning and wanted to know if I was a member of that ministry heading to the morning meeting.”

“You didn’t even talk to him.” I said and added, “What was the reason he stopped our car?”

My driver responded, “You are dressed in clothing that indicates you are important and they wanted to take you into their custody to prevent your attendance at the morning meeting of the Ministry of Planning.”

That event changed the

way I dressed from then on whenever I'm out riding around through Baghdad's streets. There is a balance to looking nice, but not too nice.

After the training for the day was completed and we were on our way back to the office I noticed the streets were eerily void of traffic. It just seemed odd. There had been no message of a curfew, but the traffic was almost non-existent. Something had just happened, was about to happen, or was happening. We didn't know what to make of the situation.

We were only five minutes from our office and my driver sped down the road. All of a sudden loud gunfire began to pop all around us. We had driven right into an ambush or some kind of gunfight.

The road we were traveling passed in front of the

Iraqi Ministry of Trade and for some reason they were under attack. My personal assistant began screaming in Arabic, "*La, la, la,*" which means "No, no, no."

My driver started to pull the car over to the curb when suddenly his right foot hit the accelerator pedal and he drove right through a gun battle. With screams and panic coming from the back seat and me praying in the front seat, my driver plowed through the scene narrowly missing huge concrete barricades and barbed razor wire that lined the streets.

Even if we had wanted to turn onto a side street to avoid the conflict, we could not have done it. The razor wire was coiled tightly and strung along the road. We would have been hung up and left sitting there in the middle of the fighting with flat tires. The best thing my driver could do was speed on through and get us to safety.

After making the corner and turning onto our last street before reaching the office, all three of us were silent. No talking, no noises, nothing. The three of us were just breathing heavy.

After reaching the safety of our office parking area, I got out and walked around the car to survey the damage. There was not one bullet hole in the car. Not one!

I said to the two traveling with me, "Let's pray and thank God for His protection. There is no reason for surviving what we just drove through. God was watching out for us."

They agreed with me and we prayed.

This was an awesome time for me to call upon the

name of Almighty God. He and He alone protects and preserves His people. My Muslim driver and personal assistant had lived through a miracle of God and I shared that moment with them.

Pray—*Dear Heavenly Father, You are mighty to save. You watch out and protect your children from danger and personal attacks. We give you praise and glorify Your name because You are worthy. Reveal Yourself to the people of Iraq as the God who delivers.*

Read—*Psalm 37:12-15, "The wicked plots against the righteous, and gnashes at him with his teeth. The Lord laughs at him; for He sees his day is coming. The wicked have drawn the sword and bent their bow, to cast down the afflicted and the needy, to slay those who are* *upright in conduct. Their sword will enter their own heart, and their bows will be broken."*

Your Thoughts—

____

Chapter Four
Near Fatal Incident

Every day is unique and often brings challenges that we are ill-prepared to meet. The morning of August 15, 2007, was no different. We had a meeting to attend and as always, we depart from the *mahad* together in one car.

Today, the "we" would be my driver, personal assistant, and me. We needed to drive about 20 minutes to our meeting. As we rode together, we discussed our project proposal and did a basic dry run of possible issues that could surface during that meeting.

As we approached the office compound, we encountered newly erected metal gates. These had replaced the previous gate that was nothing more than a metal pole which could be raised and lowered as pedestrians and car traffic entered or departed.

These gates were at least fifteen feet tall and guarded by a private security force, which added to their foreboding look. All we could do was sit there showing identification and explaining our reason for gaining entrance.

After a few minutes, we were admitted through the massive metal gates and my driver proceeded up the street. My personal assistant and I jumped out of the car while the driver turned the car around and drove back down the street. He disappeared from view behind the barricaded gate. He would return for us after our meeting.

This neighborhood has many high profile people living behind such walls and fortified gates. Many of them have become my friends and often invite me to their offices for tea. More than once I have walked into a boardroom to find the executive team in serious discussion about the future of their businesses and their personal security.

To my left was the facility which housed the German Embassy. To my right was the facility which housed the Russian Embassy. Further down the street was the Embassy of Spain. This was no common neighborhood.

Dotted here and there

were small companies whose offices were located in the neighborhood because of the promise of doing business in a secure area. However, I've learned there are no truly safe areas in Iraq and especially Baghdad.

We have been under the impression the areas of Northern Iraq are safer than those areas of Central and Southern Iraq, but as I write this, terrorists with links to Al Qaeda set off multiple car bombs in the Yezidi communities near the Syrian and Turkish borders, killing an estimated 500 souls.

We have learned there are no safe zones in Iraq, just areas that are not attacked daily. Someone commented recently to me, "It's not a matter of if, but when. We Iraqis believe we are all in the 'queue' and when it is our time—it is our time."

After our project proposal meeting, my office assistant called the driver on his cell phone and asked him to return for us. Within a few minutes, he returned to the designated pick up point. We jumped in and hurried off for the return ride back to the office.

We were all talking and discussing the meeting, when I noticed my driver becoming very quiet. He is not usually so quiet and reserved. He laughs and jokes and engages me with great enthusiasm. But this time he was quiet.

I asked him if something was wrong, His reply was frightening. He said he had lived through a gunfight earlier in the day. He looked fine, so I asked him to explain.

He began to tell me of his 20 minute drive back to the office and how he had not seen a security convoy driving through one of the many roundabouts which we have in Baghdad. One of the security detail with a large caliber automatic weapon opened fire on his car. The bullets struck the front grill of the car six or seven times, causing him to come to a sudden stop.

He said he had sat stunned and scared in his seat. A crowd of Iraqis swarmed his car to learn his fate. They asked him if he was okay. Others wanted to know if he was dead. He was alive and not one bullet touched him. It was another miracle of God's miraculous protection.

He is a man who claims to be a secularist. He says he is not a practicing Muslim and religion is what is wrong with Iraq. I told him that I thought the *wrong* religion is the problem with Iraq.

I placed my hand on his

shoulder as he drove me to the scene of the shooting and prayed out loud for him. I thanked God for protecting my friend. The driver looked at me and thanked me for my love and concern.

"I believe God has a plan for your life," I said. "He protected you for some glorious purpose."

He smiled and said he thought so, too.

When we arrived at the *mahad,* I looked at the car and marveled. The security personnel who shot at my driver could have aimed to kill, but chose to shoot a little low which spared my driver's family—and us—a great loss. I'll never know who actually pulled the trigger and I really don't care. A man's life was spared and we were all glad. My driver is not yet a follower of Jesus. I'm grieved over this and pray every Monday for his understanding and salvation.

Pray—*God, even when we don't know You are actively protecting us from harm, You are! Thank you for meeting the daily needs we have.*

Read—*Psalm 91: 4, "He will cover you with His pinions, And under His wings you will seek refuge; His faithfulness is a shield and bulwark."*

Your Thoughts—

____

____

____

____

____

____

____

____

Chapter Five
The Man Who Lost Three Sons

Across the narrow street from the Embassy of Spain is a security guard's shack. This shack is large enough for three men to sit in it comfortably and monitor the comings and goings of every visitor to the embassy.

All visitors are checked plenty of times before gaining entrance to the embassy grounds. There is usually a line of people waiting their turn to enter through the gate for conducting their business. This particular day was no different.

Or so I thought…

In January, 2007, I was leading a workshop with eighty middle managers for a local telecommunications company. I needed a little sunshine and decided to go outside and sit in the sun to refresh myself and collect my thoughts.

Iraqis are a tough crowd to stand in front of as an American. Many of them had never met an American out of uniform and didn't know what to expect from this "foreign expert" who was teaching on the topic of management skills and leadership development.

It was only mid-morning and I was already exhausted, but the cool air and warm sunshine on my face felt great. I had noticed a small concrete ledge just wide enough to sit on situated below the security wall of the Embassy of Spain.

It was a busy street with people walking from one building or office complex to another. I practiced speaking Arabic with many of them and was enjoying the conversations.

The relative calm would quickly change. I was confronted by a man with an AK-47 who requested I reenter the grounds of the telecommunication company for my safety. The area had been notorious for sniper problems and car bombs. I was really enjoying the cool January air and warmth from the sun. However, I reluctantly moved back toward the compound grounds as requested.

Just moments before this security guard approached me, a disturbance had broken out in the small guard shack across the street. I had heard a loud and angry voice wailing and screaming in pain. If my Arabic language had been better I would have known he was cursing God and everyone near him.

In addition to his cursing, he had picked up a chair and threw it away from him as he continued his wild and uncontrolled behavior. I was quickly escorted back into the relative safety of the compound grounds and away from the scene.

The look on that man's face as he threw the chair and screamed in pain will never be forgotten. I also remembered noticing the firearm in his hand and the pistol on his hip. He seemed uncontrollable and inconsolable, but didn't fire his weapons. He just cursed God and everyone near him.

I learned later from a

workshop participant the full story of what had happened and why this security guard was so angry and distraught. He had just been told his son had been assassinated in front of his wife at their home in Sadr City.

As more details were made known to me, my heart broke. At first I thought maybe his son was killed in a military action, but it was a murder. The details confirmed the killing of this man's son was an act of violence perpetrated by a militia hit squad, not by a coalition military action.

He had not lost one son, but three. This was his third born son who had been killed mercilessly in front of his mother and his younger sibling. No wonder the security guard was inconsolable. He had lost children precious to him.

I wanted to comfort him

and pray with him and offer my sincere condolences for his loss, but I didn't know how or if his anger would turn to rage against me. I decided to risk the danger and walk up to this grieving father and talk with him when I left the compound later that day.

When I walked through the gate of the office grounds, I looked toward the small guard's shack, but the grieving father was gone. I could not talk with him and express my feelings. He was gone.

I told my Iraqi friend traveling with me that the security guard lost three of his sons that day. I knew the funeral expenses would be an added burden on his family. I reached into my pocket and pulled out a $100 bill and gave it to my Iraqi friend to give this man.

"Please give him this money and tell him how sorry I

am for his loss," I explained. "Express to him how I hope this small expression of assistance will take some pressure off his family."

My friend said he would be happy to do this for me. And he did.

As my personal assistant and I walked away that day, I felt sad of heart, but the feelings of trying to do something for this family gave me a good feeling as well. I had come to Iraq to love the Iraqi people and express God's love to them. I was trying to do what I could, even if it was a small gesture.

We had one more security checkpoint to walk through before we would reach our car. In front of me was the bereaved security guard surrounded by other security guards, all with weapons. Fear seemed to grip my mind and I felt paralyzed. What if he knew I was an American and wanted to take out his anger on me?

I greeted this group of men and walked through their midst feeling I would be shot in the back. I never turned around and kept walking toward the car. He didn't shoot me and I was safe.

Once at home I thought about the events of the day. Everyone in my workshop had suffered a loss in their family from the violence that Baghdad has become famous for. All the attendees were afraid, angry, depressed, and looking for answers. I knew the answer to their struggles—a personal relationship with God through Jesus Christ.

Jesus was also the solution to the grieving security guard and his family. But how could I break through the layers of mistrust and frustration the war had brought on them? Sadaam was out of power, a representative government was in place, but most of them felt cheated and marginalized.

The Iraqis with whom I related often told me they traded one tyrant for many and don't know what to do now. There is a hopelessness that permeates this society. The longer the violence continues the less hope many of them have for a better future.

Many times I have said to anyone who would listen that Iraq is looking for political solutions to spiritual problems. The answer for Iraq is spiritual. The people of Iraq need religious freedom and the opportunity to hear and respond to the gospel.

I drifted off to sleep that night praying for the people of Iraq and in particular the security guard and his family. *What must their night have been like?*

The next day I returned to the same location for another session of training. Upon entering the main street leading to the compound where I would be teaching, I noticed the bereaved security guard standing at his post. Frankly, it surprised me to see him. I thought he would be home or taking care of his son's funeral arrangements. But, there he was at his post. He stood right where I needed to pass.

I prayed for wisdom and God's strength as I wanted to say something, anything that would convey my concern and compassion. Words were not there.

As I approached him, he recognized me. He embraced me and kissed me four times on my cheek. He thanked me for my gift to which I replied in his language, “a*fwan*,” which literally means, “not at all.”

During the break time that morning, I went back outside the safety of the gate and walked to the guard shack. The guard was still on the job and invited me in to sit with him. I joined him and we talked the entire break time.

During the conversation, he told me how his son had been a hostage for several months and had just been released two days before his assassination. He said his son was released only for the purpose of being shot in front of his family as an act of cruelty.

Two fathers

He further related to me how his two older sons had also been killed by militia hit squads. He said that his heart was so heavy he could barely function. As he spoke, his voice was filled with pain and sorrow. I could hardly hold back my own tears as we sat together. We were just two fathers from different cultures who loved being dads.

The security guard then asked me to sit for a minute longer while he went to get something from his dormitory, which was nearby. I wondered what he could be getting. What did he want to show me? Maybe it was a picture of his sons. I just sat and waited for him to return.

Within a brief few minutes, he was back. In his hand were two rings. He placed them into my hand and said, "These belonged to my boys. I want you to have them."

I refused. I couldn't accept the rings that had belonged to his sons. They were precious and I didn't feel I should accept his gift.

Another security guard who also was in that small shack immediately advised, "You must accept his gift. We are a giving people and he wants you to have them or he would not have offered them to you."

I expressed my appreciation and put them in my pocket. The grieving guard hugged me and thanked me for my compassion. He even called me “habibi” (brother) before I left.

What a difference one day can make. The day before, he had suffered incalculable loss and I thought he might vent his anger at me, an American. Today, he called me brother and was my friend.

There was a spring in my step that day and it lasted for many days thereafter. I had come to Iraq to make a difference. I couldn’t change all of Iraq. I couldn’t impact the nation as a whole, but I had touched one life and a gospel seed had been planted. We are still friends and see each other frequently.

Pray—*God of mercy and grace, make me a blessing to some hurting person today. May Your perfect love be manifest in me. Give me healing words to speak and an open heart to trust You to* *provide opportunities for me to share Your Word with people so desperate for truth. You are truth. Amen.*

Read—*Psalm 126:5-6, "Those who sow in tears shall reap with joyful shouting. He who goes to and fro weeping, carrying his bag of seed, shall indeed come again with a shout of joy, bringing his sheaves with him."*

Your Thoughts—

____

____

____

____

____

____

____

____

____

____

Chapter Six
Losing a Student

Hisham was a vivacious, intelligent, young man in his early twenties. His eyes were a blue-gray and his hair was a sandy brown color. In addition to being intelligent, he was handsome.

He would come into my office regularly to talk about his plans for the future. He was preparing to graduate from dental school and looked forward to setting up his own dental office.

He couldn't wait to begin putting into practice all the things he had learned during his training program.

Just before Hisham was to enter his final term of training, his school was closed until further notice. His dreams of graduation seemed to be put on hold. Hisham would be forced to put graduation and the opening of his dental practice on the list of "future objectives."

I was amazed at his resilience and perseverance. Even though the school had closed its doors due to the threat of violence from Al Qaeda terrorists, he poured himself into learning the English language. He simply wasn't going to stop pursuing his learning goals.

Three days a week he attended our English language institute for the purpose of keeping his mind fresh and off of his delayed dreams. When he stepped into the room, all eyes were on him. He was just that bright and exuded an energy that made every one feel better about life.

Hisham was also a Christian.

One day, he stopped by my office and sat down in the chair to the right of my desk. He was very concerned.

"Sir, it is difficult to be a non-Muslim here in Iraq at this time. Before, we Christians lived in peace with our neighbors even though they were Sunni and Shi'a. We didn't make a point to ask what their Muslim persuasion was or if their family was a blended Sunni-Shi'a family. We simply got along."

He continued, "Sadaam Hussein's leadership was a topic we never discussed even with our closest friends. We were fearful of criticizing him or his family. We didn't go out of our way to make problems for ourselves or anyone. We only wanted peace and to enjoy life. Today, this has all changed."

Hisham continued relating how his father had been killed recently and he was now trying to care for his mother while continuing to complete his education. It was a difficult and often unbearable situation for him.

Hisham stated that he and his mother continued to live as normal a life as possible, going to church, going to the market, working, and attending school.

"But now," he said ominously, "We are afraid and our fear grows every day."

"Will your university reopen?" I asked. "Would you try to finish your program?"

"If the department at my university reopens, I must finish for the sake of my family."

We had prayer and asked for God's timing and blessing. It was a wonderful time for me to listen and encourage him. Hisham really shared his heart with me that day.

During the next several weeks, Hisham came and went—always upbeat and cheerful. I marveled at his positive outlook in the face of so much uncertainty.

Some days later, he triumphantly announced that his school was going to reopen soon despite the threats that were still imminent. The instructors wanted to graduate his class. In addition, everyone associated with the decision felt reasonably sure that the security forces would prevent an Al Qaeda attack on his university.

Hisham informed me he would only have to attend class two more months and he would be finished. We both said, "*Humdulaallah*" which means, "Praise the Lord."

On April 18, 2007, Hisham was enjoying a great final week of fun and being with his friends at a beautiful mountainous area. The pictures of him with his best friends showed waterfalls, hiking trails, and Hisham playing the excited soon-to-be graduate of his university.

This field trip with friends would be his last. A few days later while attending one of the last lectures and laboratory activities at this university before graduation, a bomb planted by some unknown terrorist in a locker or water cooler near the room where Hisham and fellow classmates were finishing their programs, exploded with such force nearly everyone perished in that classroom.

Hisham died instantly from wounds he received. His body was buried on April 25 after receiving a Christian funeral. The photos and video of his funeral were even more distressing because he was buried in the same clothing he was wearing the day of his death. Blood was still on his face. Hisham's body had not been prepared for burial like we would have done in the United States.

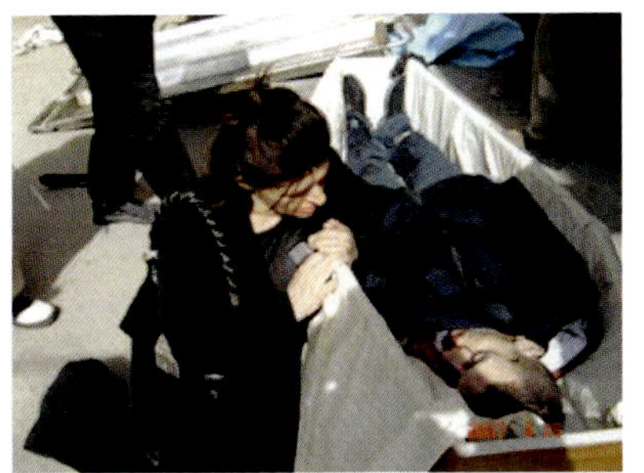

Hisham's mother letting him go

I asked one of his friends, why was he left looking like this. She said that it was to make a statement. His family wanted to show the cruelty of his death. I don't think I've ever seen a sadder funeral in my life. We were all so grieved by his death.

Someone with access to the university had sneaked into the school's hallways and hidden an explosive device near Hisham's classroom. This perpetrator strategically acted in such a way that many students and faculty lost their lives. They conveyed a message to the administration by their actions letting them know that they could get them any time the wanted.

I have personally lost more than 125 friends during my time in Baghdad, Iraq. Some were students and others were participants in my workshops. My consolation in Hisham's death was that he was a follower of Jesus and expressed his Christianity publicly and with great enthusiasm.

I don't think he was a wild-eyed risk taker. On the contrary, he simply wanted to continue living life to the fullest extent possible.

Like many Iraqis caught in the daily chaos and violence, they live by the saying, "Life goes on."

[Even as I sit here in my

Baghdad office preparing this manuscript for the printer my office assistant describes a similar event at her daughter's school just days ago. A car bomb exploded on the sidewalk out in front of her daughter's school sending shards of glass throughout the classrooms. My office assistant's daughter was seated in the first row by the windows. Glass covered the girls but no one was killed. Her daughter is my little girls only friend in Baghdad and had been in my home for a sleepover the night before this car bomb exploded. It seems to never end. March 17, 2008]

Pray—*Most kind and gracious Heavenly Father, help me to make the most of every day. You know my rising in the morning and my retiring in the evening. You order my steps and direct my life. I belong to You and live to honor You. Give me wisdom to choose the best over the good and the right over the wrong.*

Read—*Psalm 90:12, "So teach us to number our days, that we may present to You a heart of wisdom."*

Your Thoughts—

Chapter Seven
Iraqi Father for a Week

My organization's Baghdad office had been working for some time to provide an English language experience for fifty Iraqi students. These young Iraqi boys would represent their communities and would be hand-selected by the Iraqi Ministry of Sports and Youth to attend the first-ever English/Sports Camp. It was considered by many to be an honor to be selected. It also provided a chance for the boys to forget the turmoil of their neighborhoods.

The first day was a bit chaotic as boys from various backgrounds were thrust into relationships with other Iraqi boys they did not know or trust. We did not specify any specific selection criteria related to their backgrounds. Our goal was to give these boys a chance to play some sports and improve their English language competency.

Fifty boys were set loose for a week in the International Zone to run, play, and learn. What a golden opportunity. And they took full advantage of every minute.

Our volunteers came from various military and U.S. State Department offices. We had the Federal Bureau of Investigation (FBI) represented as well as other American citizens to join in the fun. My personal Iraqi staff lived with the boys in a hotel inside the International Zone and supervised them for the week-long events.

Every morning, I asked my Iraqi staff how things were going at the hotel. One morning as the week progressed, I asked the question again, “How are things at the hotel?” I was told, “Well sir, the boys are staying up all night.”

“Why?” I asked.

The answer was hilarious.

“The boys are staying up all night because many of them have never had so much electricity and running water. The boys are enjoying the air conditioning and the showers. They simply are having the times of their lives.”

One afternoon, one of the young Iraqi boys ran up to me during our baseball clinic and said to me, “My father was killed last year and I've missed him every day. This week you are my father."

He gave me a great big hug and held on for almost a minute. I embraced him in return and told him I was honored for him to call me father for the week.

After that, every time he was at bat or fielded a great play, I cheered him on as I would my own children. He constantly watched me to make sure I was keeping my eye on his playing.

There are hundreds and thousands of orphaned Iraqi children scattered around Iraq. Many of these children are housed in orphanages that do not adequately provide for their care. The money and materials given for their welfare is often stolen, misused, or sold on the local market by the directors and caregivers because they are also suffering.

I can't excuse the behavior of these caregivers, but I do understand the stress and strain they feel. Surviving in Iraq takes almost all of one's time with little left to serve or give to others.

Life is difficult, but at least one Iraqi boy had a father for a week.

Pray—*God, show me how I may minister to the needs of those less fortunate than me. My life, my resources, and my time belong to You. Give me a burden and passion to meet the emotional, spiritual and physical needs of others who are lonely, hungry, and frightened.*

Read—*James 1:27, "This is pure and undefiled religion in the sight of our God and Father, to visit orphans and widows in their* *distress, and to keep oneself unstained by the world."*

Your Thoughts—

____

____

____

____

____

____

____

____

____

Chapter Eight
My Neighbor is Missing

Several months after our arrival in Baghdad, our little family felt comfortable in our neighborhood. We enjoyed getting to know our neighbors and really talking about things that impacted our lives. Things like, "Do you have water today?" Or, "Did you have electricity last night at your house?"

One thing I never felt comfortable asking people was what they did for a living. Many of them worked with the coalition forces or U.S. sponsored relief and development projects. Knowing information like this could inadvertently get someone hurt. Most of the conversations were fairly superficial and non-intrusive relationship-builders.

One of my neighbors was the exception. Sebastian was what Iraqis called an international, who had moved to Baghdad from a South Asian country. He was open in his conversations with me and I, also, felt at ease with him. We would often visit together in the evenings talking about our projects and the difficulties involved with trying to get a project completed. We found much in common to discuss, simply by working in a place where it is so very challenging. We would always encourage each other.

This went on for several months. Then, one day, I noticed a very nice sport utility vehicle in Sebastian's yard. I went across the street to ask him about his new vehicle. It was a beautiful SUV. I was concerned about my neighbor driving it, because it looked like the many government vehicles on the road in Iraq. The problem was that these had become the focus of aggressive ambush tactics by the terrorists.

Sebastian assured me he was in no danger by reminding me that he was married to a local *Iraqiya* and he could speak Arabic fluently, the national language of Iraq. He said he could talk his way out of problems if they popped up.

About two weeks after my neighbor started driving this SUV for his work, I did not see him again. This wasn't unusual, as we both traveled all over the country to do our jobs. We had also gone for other lengths of time not talking to or seeing one another.

When a third week went by, I began to be concerned. One morning I went out to check our generator and saw one of my neighbor's co-workers in their yard. So, being a little curious, I asked where the "boss" was. The news was horrible.

This coworker only spoke Arabic very rapidly and I am far from fluent. I had to figure out what he was trying to say by the way he motioned and expressed himself emotionally as talked with me. He raised his hands into the air and said, "*Allah Kareem*" which means, "God is merciful." I had heard this before—especially after a car bomb or suicide bomber had killed not only himself, but other people in a crowded market.

There was a one million dollar ransom demand for Sebastian's safe return. It turned out that although negotiations were on-going, no one had that kind of money in our business of relief and development.

I prayed for Sebastian day and night for three months before one day receiving a phone call from him. I immediately recognized his voice.

"Hello, Brandt. This is Sebastian."

"Sebastian!" I shouted into the phone. "Where are you? Are you okay?"

His voice was soft, weak.

"I am home. Can you come see me?"

I told him that I'd be right there.

Leaving the *mahad* quickly, I headed toward Sebastian's home, but not alone. Two of my men accompanied me, just in case I was being set up for a kidnapping myself.

When we arrived at his home, one of Sebastian's co-workers escorted us into the living room. We were told to sit down and wait. I was a little nervous because I had yet to see my friend.

In a few minutes Sebastian walked into the room and asked me not to talk very much about his situation until his co-worker left. I waited patiently, still very concerned.

After a few minutes of general conversation, his co-worker left and my friend broke down in front of me and my two men.

"I think I was set up by my own co-workers," whispered Sebastian. "I don't trust them any more."

As we talked, he began to share that he and another man

had stopped at a checkpoint north of Baghdad. As they showed their identification cards to the police, terrorists came from out of nowhere.

Sebastian and the other man were dragged from their SUV and told to get into an awaiting vehicle parked over to one side of the checkpoint. They were blindfolded and their hands were bound with silver duct tape. Their legs were quickly bound, as well.

Sebastian told me he once thought they could escape, but they didn't know where to run. They remained in the back of the vehicle and were driven out to a farm just 20 minutes from the checkpoint where they had been taken hostage.

Soon after arriving at the farm, my friend said he was dragged to a place that had been dug into the ground. The hole was six feet deep and then spread out underground for about nine feet.

He was let out of the hole two times a day during his 90 days while being held hostage—once in the morning and once in the evening.

"It was horrible," he said. "They kept insisting the ransom was going to be paid and I was to be held until it was paid."

Finally, after three months of living in that hole, he was released into the custody of a police officer near the place where he was captured. The ransom had been negotiated down to $300,000.

The police returned his cell phone and personal items to him. They prepared a lunch for him while he waited for someone to come and get him.

What he said next sent chills all over me.

Not only did he suspect his own staff had set him up, he had become convinced that the local authorities were in on the kidnapping! He recognized the voice of several police in the village and knew he had heard their voices during his ordeal.

As he prepared to leave after the handover, he suggested a group picture to include the police and him standing next to one another as a parting souvenir. Once safely out of their control and back in Baghdad, he planned to use that picture from his cell phone camera as evidence to seek justice.

This is where he asked me for assistance. Since he assumed that I must know US Embassy personnel, he asked if I could put him in touch with the proper authorities.

I only knew of one person to call. Gailia, Amber, and I had

sat for hours in the airport in Amman, Jordan, a few weeks earlier waiting for our return flight to Baghdad with some Americans. It happened that there was a woman in the departure lounge from Tennessee who worked in the US Embassy. She had given us her card and asked us to call her if we needed help in the future with anything.

I returned to the *mahad* and began digging through my desk for her card. I found it and gave her a call. I asked if she remembered us and she did. She was kind and asked what she could do for me.

I explained to her the kidnapping and release of my neighbor, Sebastian. She said, "Brandt, I need to pass this information along through the proper chain. I'll be in touch soon."

After that, I called

Sebastian and told him to wait until I got word about his next step in getting justice. We prayed together again and I don't think I've ever heard a more sincere prayer. My neighbor was a believer and had developed a prayer life while in that hole that would touch the sincerity of most Christians.

The next day I received a call from the US Embassy. I answered the phone and was greeted by a staff member to our US ambassador. The staff member told me that I would soon be contacted by the FBI. He said to expect that they will ask for some information, but promised to help my friend.

The FBI did call to ask questions. I provided them with what I knew and asked them if we could set up a meeting to resolve this situation. They agreed.

The next day, Sebastian and I entered the International Zone together and prepared for the meeting. It was the most incredible thing I've witnessed up to that point living in Baghdad.

My neighbor had actually prepared a CD of the pictures he took with his cell phone to give to the FBI. Within one week. Sebastian was on a military helicopter flying back up to the area where he was seized to pinpoint the exact location where he had been held hostage.

Several insurgents were taken into custody and the corrupt police were taken into custody as well. This was one of the rare moments where justice prevailed in Iraq and I got to be a witness to that justice.

Today, Sebastian is living safely in another country with his wife and child. I may never see him again until we meet in heaven, but it is okay, just knowing that he is safe.

I witnessed God's protection and concern for my neighbor as well as answering my prayers. When I think of all the situations from which God has protected me, I marvel. What a great God I serve.

Pray—*Dear Lord, You are the protector of our lives. We humbly ask for Your will to be done in our lives. Even when evil men devise plans to harm us, You are still in control. Nothing can interfere with Your plans for our lives unless You allow it. Give us strength to live each day with confidence in You.*

Read—*Proverbs 6:16-19, "There are six things which the Lord hates, yes, seven which are* *an abomination to him: haughty eyes, a lying tongue, and hands that shed innocent blood, a heart that devises wicked plans, feet that run rapidly to evil, a false witness who utters lies, and one who spreads strife among brothers."*

Your Thoughts—

____

____

____

____

____

____

____

____

____

____

—— Epilogue ——

I first visited Iraq in October 2005 never thinking God would lead our family to actually live and work in this part of the Middle East. Life in Iraq is hard, very hard. There isn't a day where lives are not changed by the radical views of the extremists.

My father used to tell me as a child growing up, "the safest place to be is in God's will." As much as I respect the wisdom of my father, I disagree with that statement. It should be, "the best place to be is in God's will."

The world is becoming

more hostile to authentic Christianity. I think this is due in part to the *demonic entrenchment* that has occupied so many nations enslaving entire cultures for thousands of years. This demonic entrenchment we are now identifying and experiencing has created a sense of *demonic desperation* resulting in spiritual warfare unprecedented in the past as an ever expanding force of men and women of faith move into the domain of evil.

If we think Satan will voluntarily relinquish territory because we show up with the Gospel—we are fooling ourselves. The strongholds and the political and spiritual gatekeepers in the last frontier areas are going to be won for Christ by much sacrifice.

About the Author

C. Brandt Smith, Jr., is well-known and in demand as a speaker across America. He has the unique ability to apply his ready wit not only to educate and entertain, but also to drive home truths from the Bible. His experiences while traveling and living in a number of international cultures have helped not only shape his personality and worldview, but also his love for the United States.

Brandt and Gailia, have

been married twenty-seven years. They have four children and two grandchildren. Their two sons and two daughters have benefited from living abroad most of their lives.

Brandt and Gailia have served in non-Western cultures for more than fifteen years. The Mandarin Chinese language is their second language and has contributed to a major part of their ability to connect with nationals while living in China, Taiwan, and Thailand. Their work has taken them to nearly every country in East and Southeast Asia as well as many Middle Eastern countries.

He has been very active in assisting the production of the Following Jesus Mandarin version affiliated with the Chronological Oral Bible. Readers are encouraged to investigate this project at www.fjseries.org for more information.

Brandt has served on the staff of five Southern Baptist churches and was visiting adjunct professor of missions for Mid-America Baptist Theological Seminary and Williams Baptist College.

Brandt, Gailia, and their daughter, Amber, lived in Baghdad for two years beginning in 2006 until 2008 where he served as country director for an non-governmental organization.

Another publication by the same author, "Lookout for the Headhunters!" is also available through www.brandtsmithpublishing.com and www.amazon.com. Just type in the author's name for quick access.